BASIC/NOT BORING
LANGUAGE SKILLS

READING COMPREHENSION

Grades 4-5

Inventive Exercises to Sharpen
Skills and Raise Achievement

Series Concept & Development
by Imogene Forte & Marjorie Frank

Exercises by Marjorie Frank

Illustrations by Kathleen Bullock

Incentive Publications, Inc.
Nashville, Tennessee

Thank you to the fourth and fifth graders who contributed pieces of original writing to be used in this book, and additional thanks to poet David May, who inspired many of the writers during his sessions with them as a "Poet in Residence" at Briscoe and Helman Schools in Ashland, Oregon. These pieces are used by permission from the writers.

page 21   Paul Ireland for *"Magic"*

page 28   Tahli O'Grady for *"The Terror of the Wind"*

page 29   Laura Arndt for *"Life is Like"*
             Camille Morris for *"Life is Like"*
             Kate Bridges for *"Your Room is Like"*

page 37   Kathryn Harriss for *"Something's Coming"*
             Linda NewComb for *"Far From Civilization"*

Page 58   Ashley Roda for *"I Hear"*
             Chloe Hansen for *"I Hear"*
             Tessah Joseph for *"What I Hear"*
             Christopher Bingham for *"Silence"*

page 59   Sophie DiStefano for *"What I WAS and What I AM"*
             Joseph Zoline-Black for *"The Wind"*

About the cover:
> Bound resist, or tie dye, is the most ancient known method
> of fabric surface design. The brilliance of the basic tie dye
> design on this cover reflects the possibilities that emerge
> from the mastery of basic skills.

Cover art by Mary Patricia Deprez, dba Tye Dye Mary®
Cover design by Marta Drayton, Joe Shibley, and W. Paul Nance
Edited by Anna Quinn

ISBN 0-86530-399-1

PRINTED IN THE UNITED STATES OF AMERICA

TABLE OF CONTENTS

CELEBRATE BASIC LANGUAGE SKILLS

Basic does not mean boring! There certainly is nothing dull about . . .

    . . . joining Pecos Bill and learning to lasso a speeding train

    . . . taking a ride on the *Orient Express* right in the middle of a mystery

    . . . diving to explore the sunken *Titanic* or venturing into the Bermuda Triangle

    . . . coming face-to-face with the Loch Ness monster

    . . . learning to make a mummy or climb the Empire State Building

    . . . wrestling an alligator or fighting a fierce bull

    . . . searching for mermaids and the lost city of Atlantis

    . . . visiting a rock concert in the Stone Age or in the year 3000

These are just some of the adventures students can explore as they celebrate basic language skills. The idea of celebrating the basics is just what it sounds like—enjoying and improving the skills of reading. Each page invites learners to try a high-interest, appealing exercise that will sharpen one or more specific reading skills. This is no ordinary fill-in-the-blanks way to learn! These exercises are fun and surprising. Students will do the useful work of practicing reading skills while they enjoy fascinating adventures in the past, present, or future. They can travel with a clever Adventure Company and try adventures that are real, fantastic, or just plain outrageous! At the same time they practice basic reading skills, they'll also be sharpening thinking skills and many other language skills.

The pages in this book can be used in many ways:
- to sharpen or review a reading skill with one student
- to reinforce the skill with a small or large group
- by students working on their own
- by students working under the direction of a parent or teacher

Each page may be used to introduce a new skill, to reinforce a skill, or to assess a student's performance of a skill. And there's more than just the great student activity pages. You'll also find an appendix of resources helpful to students and teachers—including a ready-to-use test for assessing reading skills. The pages are written with the assumption that an adult will be available to assist the students with their learning and practice.

As your students take on the challenges of these adventures with reading, they will grow! And as you watch them check off the basic language skills they've strengthened, you can celebrate with them!

The Skills Test

Use the skills test beginning on page 57 as a pretest and/or a post-test. This will help you check the students' mastery of basic reading skills and will prepare them for success on achievement tests.

SKILLS CHECKLIST FOR
READING COMPREHENSION, Grades 4-5

✔	SKILL	PAGE(S)
	Determine word meaning from context	10–14
	Recognize and use synonyms	10–14
	Recognize and use antonyms	10, 11
	Gain information from reading titles and captions	15–17, 21
	Identify cause-effect relationships	16
	Read to find answers to questions	17–19, 21–23, 25–28, 35–43, 46–54
	Identify literal and implied main ideas	18, 19
	Distinguish between facts and opinions	20
	Read to find details and information	20–54
	Identify supporting details	21–27
	Choose the best title for a selection	21
	Paraphrase or summarize a written text	24, 32–34
	Identify literary techniques used to enhance written pieces	28, 29
	Identify figurative language; describe its effect on the writing	29
	Determine sequence of events	30, 31
	Draw logical conclusions from written material	34, 35, 39, 43
	Make generalizations based on material read	35, 39
	Identify the author's point of view and purpose	36, 37
	Predict future actions or outcomes	38, 39
	Use information gained from text to make inferences	38, 40
	Evaluate ideas, conclusions, or opinions from a text	41, 42
	Analyze characters used in written pieces	43–45
	Identify elements of a story (setting, plot, characters, theme)	44, 45
	Make use of illustrations or graphics to understand a text	46–52
	Identify incorrect details in a passage	47
	Supply missing information for a passage	47
	Interpret charts and tables	48, 49
	Interpret and make graphs	50, 51
	Read to follow directions	51, 52
	Explain personal responses to written material	53, 54

READING COMPREHENSION

Skills Exercises

ADVENTURES, UNLIMITED!

Let us take you on the adventure of your dreams! **Adventures, Unlimited** is the one stop when you are shopping for travel anywhere, anytime. We have special trips to real and fantasy locations in the past, present, and future! Choose your adventure—and start packing!

Global EXUBERANCE passport Explore beautiful soar
Travel new Wonders

TIME-TRAVEL ADVENTURES

Attend a masked ball at palace Versailles.
Learn to make a mummy in ancient Egypt.
Take a gander at Camelot.
Comb the streams for gold with the '49ers.
Test-drive a car of the future!
Drop in on Leonardo da Vinci.
Celebrate a Stone Age Rock Concert.
Rock with music groups of the far future.

EXPEDITIONS INTO WIND & WATER

Ride the world's most colossal waves.
Snoop around the ruins of the Titanic.
Raft through treacherous whitewater.

FANTASY ADVENTURES

Fraternize with the real Mother Goose.
Make friends with Paul Bunyan.
Try wild escapades with Pecos Bill.
Scrutinize clues with the legendary Sherlock Holmes.
Take a ride in Elvis's lavish Rolls Royce.

Different LITER customs
tickets Magic
vacations Heart

Find a word on the adventure posters that matches each direction below.
Look on both pages (pages 10 and 11).

Find a word that is a synonym for . . .

1. adventure _____

2. sail _____

3. tricks _____

4. socialize _____

5. examine _____

6. try _____

7. travel _____

Use with page 11.

Find 2 synonyms for *search*

8. _____

_____

Find a word or phrase that means . . .

9. make-believe _____

10. grand _____

11. having to do
    with food _____

12. climb _____

Name _____

Space Mountain Dream

Fabulous

OUTRAGEOUS EXPEDITIONS

Take off on an escapade to the Mir Space Station.
Camp alone in the dark, foreboding forest.
Endeavor to climb the Empire State Building.

Creature Escapades!

Catch an elusive Leprechaun.
Face the fiercest bull.
Search for a mythical mermaid.

REAL EXCITEMENT IN REAL PLACES

Probe the world's deepest cavern.
Spend a month at Clown College.
Learn downhill antics from Olympic Champions.
Scale the great Denali Mountain.
Sail the highest, wildest seas.
Compete in the Iditarod.
Helicopter to ski the remote Alps.
Engage a ride on the Orient Express.

IMAGINE EXUBERANCE

GREAT

Modern

BARGAIN ADVENTURES

Rule the court for a day.
Learn to soar through the air on a pole.
Eat your way to a culinary world record.

mother nature

perfect

GREAT MYSTERY ADVENTURES

Search for the lost city of Atlantis.
Venture into the Bermuda Triangle, if you dare.
Meet the unfathomable Loch Ness Monster.

Holy Cow!

QUEST vacation Echoes

Find a word on the adventure posters that matches each direction below.

Write a word that is an antonym for . . .

13. safe_____

14. real_____

15. modern _____

16. pleasant_____

17. small_____

18. plain & simple_____

19. believable _____

20. past_____

Write a word that is a synonym for . . .

21. hard to catch _____

22. famous_____

23. wreck_____

24. a good price _____

25. hire_____

26. a look_____

27. far away_____

28. scariest_____

Use with page 10.

Name _____

LIGHTS REQUIRED

ADVENTURE #1 Explore the Réseau Jean Bernard Cave, the deepest cave in the world. Bring a hard hat, wear a raincoat, and don't forget the lights!

Decide what the words below the dialogue balloons mean in the context of the conversation. Write the meaning.

1. ludicrous _____   4. penetrated _____

2. elated _____   5. rue _____

3. cavern _____   6. sodden _____

7. precarious _____   10. carping _____

8. hiatus _____   11. disquieted _____

9. thwart _____   12. sinister _____

What do you think will happen next in the cave? _____

_____

Name _____

NO LICENSE NECESSARY

Adventure #2 We'll sneak you into the secret showroom of one of the top car companies to see some cars for the future. Then you can hop right into the car of your choice and take it for a test-drive!

Read the rules for test-driving this awesome vehicle. Tell what each word listed below means. Decide its meaning from seeing how it is used in the rules list.

RULES for TEST-DRIVERS

#1 Drivers must certify that they are over age 10.

#2 Never render body safety restraints inoperable.

#3 Submit to all instructions given by the computer.

#4 Do not deploy parachutes at speeds under 70 mph.

#5 No ingesting of liquids at speeds over 200 mph.

#6 Do not eat pizza or other lardaceous foods in the car.

#7 Do not deposit or throw refuse in the car.

#8 Drivers are precluded from watching the movie system.

#9 Attend to information disseminated by the computer.

#10 This model is banned from the mono-rail systems.

#11 Do not tamper with automatic speed control devices.

#12 Drivers showing excessive aggression will be chastened.

#13 Any traffic citations will be charged to the driver.

#14 This car must be promptly returned at termination of drive.

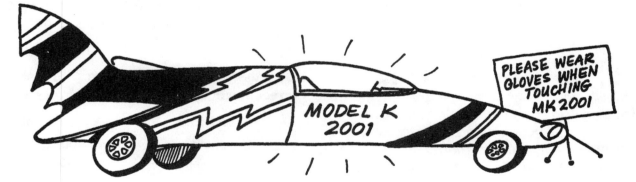

1. certify _____

2. render _____

   inoperable _____

3. submit _____

4. deploy _____

5. ingesting _____

6. lardaceous _____

7. refuse _____

8. precluded _____

9. attend _____

   disseminated _____

10. banned _____

11. tamper _____

12. excessive _____

   chastened _____

13. citations _____

14. promptly _____

   termination _____

Name _____

CURES & COURAGE

ADVENTURE #3 Venture into the largest swamp in the world—the deep, damp Everglades. Take a swamp boat up the river to see the swamp creatures. If you're ready, we'll give you an alligator-wrestling lesson, too! You'll need a good dose of courage to try this! If you run into trouble, maybe the cures below will help you.

PREVENTING ALLIGATOR BITES

Endeavor to avoid alligator bites at all costs. **Appease** the alligator with the offer of a bag of rippled potato chips before you start the wrestling match. As a **precautionary** measure, get yourself an alligator-proof suit that is too thick for alligator teeth to **penetrate**. Of course, the **surefire** way to avoid bites is to avoid the alligator!

HOW TO HEAL ALLIGATOR BITES

If an alligator bites you, mix the juice of 12 tomatoes with cooked oatmeal. Squeeze in 7 drops of root beer. Spread this over the **affected** area right away. Then cover the area with warm banana peels and wrap **securely** with plastic wrap. After just an hour, the bite will be **substantially** on its way to healing.

CURE for WARTS

If you end up with warts after an **encounter** with an alligator, you'll be in need of this potion. Pick 3 fresh cabbages. Slice them and drop them in a blender with 2 cups of chocolate milk. Sprinkle in a handful of **tangy** chili powder. Add a **dollop** of mustard and a tablespoon of vinegar to the mixture and blend for 2 minutes at high speed. Drink this at bedtime and sleep for 12 hours. When you awake, the warts will be gone.

CURE for a HEADACHE

It's not uncommon to have a **throbbing** headache after a good wrestling match. The best cure is a good old-fashioned onion wrap. Boil 20 onions in 2 quarts of water for an hour. Add ½ cup of molasses. Soak some old rags in the liquid for several minutes. When they are **saturated**, squeeze out the juice and **envelop** your head with the rags. Sit very still in a **dark** room, and your headache will **vanish** for sure in 15 minutes.

Match the words from the cures with their correct meanings. Use the context to help you.

____ 1. endeavor	a. considerably
____ 2. appease	b. pounding
____ 3. precautionary	c. disappear
____ 4. penetrate	d. try
____ 5. surefire	e. spicy
____ 6. affected	f. soaked
____ 7. securely	g. preventive
____ 8. substantially	h. enter
____ 9. encounter	i. satisfy
____ 10. tangy	j. wrap
____ 11. dollop	k. large drop
____ 12. throbbing	l. tightly
____ 13. saturated	m. foolproof
____ 14. envelop	n. hurt
____ 15. vanish	o. meeting

Name

LESSONS IN SILLINESS

Adventure #4 Spend a month at Clown College. Yes, clowns go to school to learn the silly stuff they do! Go to a clown college, too, and learn a lot about clowning around! Read the titles of the books that would-be clowns must read in college. Then follow the directions below.

Write the letter of the book in which you would expect to learn each of these things:

_____ 1. how to make clown faces

_____ 2. complicated jokes

_____ 3. how to keep from injuring your back during somersaults

_____ 4. jokes, when you know none

_____ 5. how to choose your first costume

_____ 6. what to do about a bad rash on your nose

_____ 7. how to make your nose look great

_____ 8. how to fix a flat tire on your unicycle

_____ 9. tricks to do with balloons

_____ 10. funny ways to move your body

_____ 11. how to walk with big feet

_____ 12. why clowns have big feet

_____ 13. how to get nine clowns on a skateboard

_____ 14. getting makeup out of your eyes

A. CLOWN NOSES EVERYTHING YOU NEED TO KNOW

B. The Complete Collection of BEST JOKES Beginner to Advanced

C. Creative Costumes

D. the 300 WORST CLOWNING INJURIES Prevention Guide

E. a short history of BIG Feet!

F. Unicycle maintenance A 12-STEP MANUAL

G. A CLOWN'S HAND BOOK OF TRICKS

H. MAKEUP GUIDE FOR UNIQUE CLOWN FACES

Name

OLD NEWS IS GOOSE NEWS

Adventure #5 Was there really a Mother Goose? Yes, there was! Was this Mother Goose the one who started all the nursery rhymes? Visit the eighteenth-century home of Mother Goose in Boston, and find out for yourself!

Read each headline that has come straight from one of Mother Goose's rhymes. The headlines give a result or effect of something that has happened. For each newspaper, choose the sentence that you think tells the cause of each headline.

1
Paws Tribune
Morning Edition
KITTENS SUFFER FROM COLD PAWS

a. They forgot their mittens.
b. They got their mittens.
c. They hid from their mother.

2
LAMB'S GAZETTE
BAA BAA BLACK SHEEP HAS EMPTY BAGS

a. He never had any wool.
b. He hasn't bought the wool yet.
c. He gave away his three bags of wool.

3
Daily News
Spider Is Washed Out

a. Itsy Bitsy went up the waterspout.
b. The sun came out.
c. The rain came down.

4
Quickston Evening News
JACK JUMPS QUICKLY

a. He's in a hurry to get to bed.
b. He's jumping over a hot flame.
c. He's training for a hurdle race.

5
Evening News
PORRIDGE TURNS COLD

a. Porridge was never hot.
b. The porridge has been in the pot for nine days.
c. The porridge burned in the pot.

6
Country Daily News
FARMER'S WIFE CUTS TAILS OFF MICE

a. The mice ate her cheese.
b. The mice were blind.
c. The mice chased the farmer's wife.

7
Peckland Gazette, July 19
PETER PIPER IS WORN OUT

a. Peter blew his horn all night.
b. Peter went to market.
c. Peter picked a peck of pickled peppers.

8
Goose Gazette, Thursday
JACK BREAKS HEAD OPEN

a. Jack went up the hill.
b. Jack fell down the hill.
c. Jill came tumbling after.

Name

TRICKS ON THE SLOPES

ADVENTURE #6 Learn downhill tricks from the champions! All kinds of fantastic antics happen on the slopes in the Winter Olympic Games. Here's your chance to learn some tricks from the best athletes!

Read the caption beside each picture. Then answer the questions. If the captions do not supply an answer, write NA (for not applicable).

1. In the halfpipe event, snowboarders zip up and down the steep sides of a halfpipe. It is a U-shaped trench carved out of snow. Halfpipe competitors do wild tricks with crazy names like Ollies, Chicken Salad, McTwist, and Fakies.

3. Aerial skiing contests are great fun! Daring skiers perform flips and twists in the air off a 66-yard long ramp. Judges give them a score that is based 20% on the takeoff, 50% on the flight in the air, and 30% on the landing.

2. USA's Picabo Street won a silver medal in downhill racing at the 1994 Olympics. Then she injured her knee badly in 1996, but came back to win a gold medal in the Super-Giant Slalom at the 1998 games in Japan.

4. Ski jumpers fly through the air with their ski-tips spread apart in a V-style. This V gives them greater lift from the air as the air flows beneath the skis. This helps the skiers fly farther. Nasahiko Harada, from Japan, is one of the best ski jumpers ever.

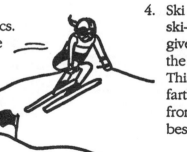

1. In which three sports are athletes jumping into the air? _____

2. Why do ski jumpers use a V-style in the air? _____

3. Which sport has a trick named Chicken Salad? _____

4. How much of an aerial skier's score is based on the landing? _____

5. For what event did Picabo Street win a medal in 1994? _____

6. What is the sport of Japan's Nasahiko Harada? _____

7. In which two sports shown do athletes do twists? _____

8. How high in the air do aerial skiers perform? _____

9. When did Picabo Street injure her knee? _____

10. What is a halfpipe? _____

11. How long is the ramp for aerial skiing? _____

Name _____

THE MYSTERIOUS ATLANTIS

Adventure #7 Climb aboard a submarine to search the oceans for the lost city of Atlantis. People wonder if Atlantis really existed. You can help to solve the mystery once and for all!

1.

Atlantis was a large mythical island in the Atlantic Ocean. Plato, a writer in ancient Greece, wrote a tale about this island. The tale told of a great empire that existed on Atlantis. In the tale, earthquakes, floods, and great storms shook the whole island. During the great storms, the island sank into the sea.

The main idea of this paragraph is
a) Plato was a great writer.
b) Atlantis is a mythical island that disappeared into the sea.
c) Many tales have been told about Atlantis.
d) Earthquakes have destroyed many islands in the ocean.

2.

For centuries, people were fascinated with Plato's tales about the island of Atlantis. Many wondered where it was and how it sank. Many wondered if it was a real place or just another Greek myth. Perhaps it really existed at one time. Over the years, many stories and fantasies have been told about a great city that lies beneath the ocean. Some think that it is still inhabited by sea creatures such as mermaids and mermen. Some scientists think the tales were inspired by a real island, the island of Thira in the Aegean Sea. This island was destroyed by a volcanic eruption in 1500 B.C.

The main idea of this paragraph is
a) There are many questions and theories about the existence and fate of Atlantis.
b) Many people think sea creatures still live in Atlantis.
c) The island of Atlantis was destroyed by a volcano.

3.

The great mythical empire of Atlantis was built on an island in the Atlantic Ocean. Atlantis had powerful armies which planned to conquer all of the lands in the Mediterranean area. They had success in parts of Europe and North Africa, but the armies of Athens defeated them and drove them away.

The main idea of this paragraph is
a) Atlantis had powerful armies.
b) Athens had powerful armies.
c) Armies of Atlantis tried to conquer other lands.

Name

MYTHICAL SEA CREATURES

Adventure #8 Wouldn't you like to find a mermaid? Join the hunt! Keep your eyes open, and you might catch a glimpse of these fantastic creatures!

Read the diary entries of one adventurer who went on this trip last summer. Write the main idea for each of her entries.

Thursday, May 18

Dear Diary,
Today I joined the crew of the submarine named *Explorer*. We are going on a hunt for mermaids. I have wanted to do this all my life. I am so excited! I hope I see one!
Maria

The main idea is_____
_____
_____

Saturday, May 20

Dear Diary,
I've been learning about the history of mermaids today. Irish legends say that mermaids were women who did not follow the religion of their day in Ireland. Because of this, they were banished from the earth by St. Patrick. The only place they had to live was in the sea.
Maria

The main idea is_____
_____
_____

Tuesday, May 22

Dear Diary,
Along with their belief in mermaids, many people in Ireland and Scotland believe in sea serpents. There are frequent reports of people sighting them. These are huge sea snakes that are about 300 feet long. Stories of the Scottish Loch Ness monster and the kraken of Scandinavia have been told for years. I'm hoping to see a sea serpent, too!
Maria

The main idea is_____
_____
_____

Friday, May 25

Dear Diary,
How thrilling! I am just sure I saw a mermaid today. She had the head and body of a woman. Below the waist, the creature was a fish with scales and a long tail. Really! I did see one swimming off the side of the boat!
Maria

The main idea is_____
_____
_____

Name _____

SPACE MISSION

ADVENTURE #9 Fly a shuttle through space to visit the Space Station *Mir*. This is the place where astronaut Shannon Lucid set an American space duration record in 1996. You don't have to stay as long as she did!

Read the travel brochure for the station. Use red to circle all statements that are facts. Use blue to circle all statements that are opinions.

You'll be so glad you did this!!

VISIT MIR
SPACE STATION

Travel to Mir by Space Shuttle

- Orbit the Earth & see fantastic sights!
- Astronauts will enjoy your visit!
- See the 6-port docking system.
- Explore the living and working spaces.
- Get fitted with your own space suit.
- Walk in space.
- All food and equipment are provided.
- You'll love the food!
- You'll have fun feeling weightless!
- No dangers or accidents will occur.

All astronauts & cosmonauts want a chance to live on Mir!

Must be at least 25 years of age.

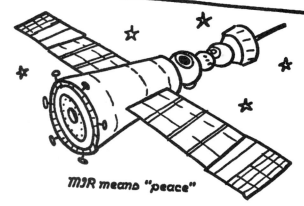

MIR means "peace"

WE PROVIDE TRAINING!

STAY 5, 10, or 15 days

We won't keep you as long as we kept Cosmonaut Aleksandr Laveikin. He stayed 326 days!

Mir was launched in 1986 by the Soviet Union. Today it is maintained by Russia.

Schedule	
TRAINING	January 1
LAUNCH	December 5
RETURN FLIGHTS	December 9
	December 14
	December 19

Adventures, Unlimited

You can afford it!
See your Adventure Company Representative

Health examination required.

Name

CATCH A LEPRECHAUN

ADVENTURE #10 Travel with us to the land of magic. Visit Ireland and hunt for those friendly little elves called leprechauns. Catch one (if you can)! Maybe you'll find a pot of gold while you're searching!

With magic you can soar in
the clouds with the angels. You can say hello to the fairies,
Fly on winged unicorns' backs, Go to the Amazon Jungle and play with
boas and black panthers, Be a wizard, a super hero, a monster, and almost
anything! You can smell the prehistoric air, create a time machine and go to
the future. Build a giant hunk of metal and create a star-ship. Be the first
boy or girl to dig to the pit of the Earth. You can
pull a bunny out of your hat, Glide
from the stars, and slide down bright,
colorful rainbows. Wherever you are,
whatever time it is, you can find magic
in your heart and you can be anything,
and do anything you may want to do!

Paul Ireland, Gr. 4

Using the poem above, finish the sentences and questions.

With magic, you can . . .

1. Say hello to _____.
2. Slide down _____.
3. Play with _____ in the Amazon.
4. Be the first to_____.
5. Pull _____ out of your hat.
6. Glide from _____.
7. Create_____.
8. Smell _____.
9. Be _____.
10. Fly on _____.
11. Where can you find magic?

_____

12. What would be the best title of the poem?
    a. Flying on Unicorns
    b. Soar with Angels
    c. Magic: Do You Believe in It?
    d. The Magic Hat

13. Which of the magic things would you like to be able to do?

_____

_____

14. What else would you do if you could work magic?

_____

_____

Name _____

20,000 FEET AND STILL CLIMBING

ADVENTURE #11 Climb the Great Denali! That's the Indian name for Mt. McKinley, the highest mountain in North America. You'll need lots of training and practice for this adventure in the center of the Alaska Mountain Range because the height of "the great one" is 20,320 feet!

Get ready for climbing by shopping for equipment and supplies.

USED EQUIPMENT
picks
sleeping bags
tents
maps
camping stoves

GREAT DEALS!
Mountain Supply
552-9900

ZOOM
HEADLAMP
Best one on the market!
$39
Saturday Only
Camping Ltd.
201 First St.

THE
ULTIMATE
TENT
See it! Try it!
100% waterproof
lightweight shelter
easy to set up in snow!
double sewn seams
weight—4 lbs
ON SALE, NOW

Climber's Shop
1000 Broad St.

CARABINERS
you can count on
New 3-D shape
Every one tested!
Lightweight!

Stop & see them!
Mountain Store
3910 Abby Lane

VIDEO
CLIMBING DENALI
See the climb before you do it!
$20.00
Video Stop Shop
550-2980

SLEEPING
BAGS
for cold places
100% fine goose down
Good to −60°
High Quality design
ALL BAGS
30% OFF

Camping, Ltd.
201 First St.

---

1. What is the weight of the ultimate tent? _____

2. Are used climbing ropes advertised? _____

3. What product is advertised as having a 3-D shape? _____

4. Which products are advertised as lightweight? _____

5. Where can you buy a product that is 100% waterproof? _____

6. What would you pay for a ZOOM headlamp and the video? _____

7. Where is the Mountain Store located? _____

8. What can you see on the advertised video? _____

9. Where can you buy maps? _____

10. What store is on First Street? _____

11. How many stores have phone numbers advertised? _____

12. What phone number would you call to ask about camping stoves? _____

13. Where can you buy carabiners? _____

14. How much money would you save on a $250 sleeping bag at Camping, Ltd? _____

15. What is the lowest temperature for the sleeping bags at Camping, Ltd? _____

Name _____

BRING YOUR AXE!

ADVENTURE #12

Are all those stories about Paul Bunyan really true? Head off into the forest and meet him for yourself. Maybe he'll teach you how to swing an axe or how to eat 37 pancakes at one sitting!

JOB APPLICATION
Position: LUMBERJACK

Name	Paul Bunyan
Age	22
Place of Birth	Maine
Height	8 feet 11 inches
Weight	344 pounds
Physical Condition	EXCELLENT
Shoe Size	200
Experience	Woodsplitting, tree felling, lumberjack work across the nation
Abilities & Qualities That Make You Fit for the Job	*great strength and endurance *can fell two trees at one blow *can swing axe 16 hours without stopping *created the Great Lakes with my footprints *5 years experience
Special Requirements	I need to eat 20,000 calories a day.
Preferred Working Conditions and Why	I prefer to work with my great blue ox, Babe. The spread of his horns is the length of 42 axe handles. He can haul great quantities of wood.

1. How tall was Paul in inches?_____

2. Whom did Paul prefer for a working partner?_____

3. If Paul worked as a lumberjack for 25 years after he got this job, how old was he when he quit?_____

4. Would you hire Paul for this job? _____

5. Why or why not? _____

6. Which quality do you think best qualified him for this job? _____

_____

7. What characteristic might make an employer hesitate to hire Paul?

_____

_____

8. If you were the employer, what question would you like to ask Paul in an interview? _____

_____

_____

9. Write a one-sentence description of Paul.

_____

_____

Name

EXPLORE THE SUNKEN TITANIC

ADVENTURE #13 Join the underwater explorers as they unlock the mysteries of this great ship, the *Titanic*.

THE VOYAGE OF THE TITANIC

They called it "unsinkable," but the *Titanic* was not. They called it a floating luxury hotel, and indeed it was! It was like a huge palace, with huge rooms, gold-plated light fixtures, a swimming pool, and steam baths. No ship this big or beautiful had ever been built before! Hundreds of passengers and families boarded the *Titanic* in Southampton, England, on April 10, 1912. The great new ship was bound for New York on its maiden voyage.

At a half hour past midnight on April 15, 1912, disaster struck the *Titanic*. Actually, the ship struck disaster—in the form of an iceberg. At first, passengers didn't realize that the accident was serious. There was a command for people to get into the lifeboats. Unfortunately, the company that built the boat was so convinced it was unsinkable that they had sent lifeboats for only about half the people on board.

The ship sent out distress signals, hoping nearby ships would come to help. The bow of the *Titanic* was sinking when a loud, roaring noise went up from the ship. The *Titanic* was breaking apart. It stood up in the air for a short while, and then disappeared beneath the waves. The next day, another ship, the *Carpathia*, came to rescue many survivors. Survivors included 712 passengers and crew members. Hundreds did not survive.

There are many theories about why the *Titanic* sank. Seventy-five years after the sinking, and after much searching, the wreckage of the *Titanic* was found. Small submarines have explored the wreckage. Maybe some of the mysteries will now be solved.

Write a one-sentence summary of the story.

_____

_____

_____

_____

Name

LETTERS TO LEONARDO

ADVENTURE #14 Grab a seat on the time machine and head back to the Italian Renaissance to meet Leonardo Da Vinci, an incredibly talented artist and scientist.

Read these fan letters to Leonardo, and then answer the questions below.

Venice, April 1489

Dear Leonardo,

I have been a fan of yours for years. You are a remarkable man. I am so impressed with your paintings, the *Mona Lisa*, which you painted in Florence in the early 1500s, and *The Last Supper*, which you painted earlier in Milan. Why did you never finish your early painting of *St. Jerome*? I wish I could meet you.

Georgio

Florence, May 1507

Dear Leonardo,

I am so impressed with your notebooks, where the most important information was put into your drawings. I hear there are over 30 of them. They are full of amazing drawings and notes about painting, architecture, human anatomy, mechanics, biology, and other things. When did you have time to write them all?

Alicia

Chicago, June 1998

Dear Leonardo,

I am surprised to learn that you drew plans for an airplane and a helicopter 300 years before flying machines were successfully built. I have also been amazed to see your perfect drawings of human anatomy. I always thought you were only an artist! But now I have learned that you were also a scientist, sculptor, architect, mathematician, military advisor, and engineer!

charlie

1. Which letter mentioned an unfinished painting? _____

2. What surprised Charlie? _____

3. Which two fans mentioned Leonardo's drawings? _____

4. Which painting was completed earlier, *Mona Lisa* or *The Last Supper?* _____

5. Which fan was excited about Leonardo's drawings of flying machines? _____

6. Where did Alicia live? _____

7. Which fan wrote his or her letter first? _____

8. Name three topics in Leonardo's notebooks. _____

Name _____

ROCK INTO THE PAST

ADVENTURE #15 Attend the very first rock concert! Take an awesome time machine into the Stone Age and get ready to rock!

1. Who performs *My Cave's on Fire?*

   _____

2. What is the closing song?

   _____

3. What follows the intermission?

   _____

4. What song does Mick Jagged & the Rolling Boulders perform?

   _____

5. Which song is sung by the Smashing Marbles?

   _____

6. Who sings with Bronto?

   _____

7. What do the Limestone Lovers perform?

   _____

8. Who is the lead singer with the Hot Rocks?

   _____

9. Who performs *The Gravel Pit Rock?*

   _____

10. Who sings about a brontosaurus?

    _____

11. Where is the concert held?

    _____

12. How many groups perform before the intermission? _____

13. Who performs *Dancin' at the Quarry?*

    _____

14. When does the concert begin?

    _____

15. Who sings about granite?

    _____

GRANITEVILLE MUSIC FEST
Place: Hard Rock Arena
Time: After Dark

PROGRAM

I Dino If I Love You Anymore
Mick Jagged & the Rolling Boulders

I Feel Like a Brontosaurus Stomped on my Head
The Petro Cliff Trio

Your Love Is Like a Sabre-Tooth Tiger
Terri Dactyl & the Hot Rocks

Sha-boom, Sha-boom, Sha-Rock
The Lava-Ettes

You're As Cuddly As a Woolly Mammoth
The Smashing Marbles

INTERMISSION

Be a Little Boulder, Honey
Curt McCave

The Gravel Pit Rock
The Cro-Magnon Crooners

Please Don't Take Me for Granite, Baby
The Standing Stones

My Cave's on Fire
The Paleo-Lyths

Your Heart's Made of Stone
Bronto & the Cave Dudes

Dancin' at the Quarry
Tommy Shale

I've Cried Pebbles over You
The Limestone Lovers

Till the Volcano Blows
The Square Wheels

Name

ROCK INTO THE FUTURE

ADVENTURE #16 Travel through time to the year 3000 for the opening night of the Far-out Concert at the Cosmic Arena. Hear songs no one else will hear for 1000 years!

Look for these literary techniques used in the sentences below. Write the code letter of each technique used in each sentence. Some sentences may have more than one.

> **A** = alliteration
> **PN** = pun
> **I** = idiom
> **M** = metaphor
> **P** = personification
> **S** = simile
> **R** = rhyme
> **E** = exaggeration

_____ 1. Rock and roll always grabs my soul.

_____ 2. That song was longer than a comet's tail.

_____ 3. That last singer is an old stick in the mud.

_____ 4. His singing is like a brilliant laser light show.

_____ 5. Oooh! That cute drummer has caught my eye.

_____ 6. Haratia's hairdo is wider than an asteroid belt.

_____ 7. Lagoola is crying her eyes out over that song.

_____ 8. Her singing is as spectacular as a meteor shower.

_____ 9. Don't you love that rollicking rock and roll rhythm?

_____ 10. Don't try to worm your way out of going to the concert.

_____ 11. Her voice is so sweet, it turns the clouds to sugared candy.

_____ 12. The heavy drumbeats wrap their fat fingers around my ears.

_____ 13. The comets in the sky shout the secrets of a thousand years.

_____ 14. Music is a banquet that feeds all species, with plenty of leftovers.

_____ 15. The music yanks me to my feet and makes me her dancing partner.

_____ 16. Six serious singing Sagook sisters swayed slowly to smooth soft sounds.

_____ 17. I hear that the guitar player has been stringing his girlfriend along for weeks

Name _____

HIGH SEAS ADVENTURE

ADVENTURE #17 Have you always wanted to get your hands on the wheel and try to steer a ship at sea? Here's your chance to be the captain of a sailing vessel. Let's hope you don't get seasick!

Read the poem about the sea. Then answer the questions.

The Terror of the Wind
by Tahli O'Grady, Gr. 3

The sea was roaring up with thunder
Up to the angry winds,
Which tore through the air dancing to and fro.
Once again the lightning slipped another cut into
    the dancing air,
Which wailed and wailed from the lightning sharp knife.
The sea kept moaning from the mountains that rose
    higher and higher as they crawled upon its back,
And again the thunder crashed through the air, trying
    to hide itself from the pounding rain,
As it poured through the air.
Then after all its strikes, the lightning's knife grew dull,
As it stabbed the sea once more.
Then the sea could no longer hold the towering mountains
    upon its back.
As the rain grew tired of falling,
It carefully settled down to lay,
As the thunder rolled back up to the sky to sleep for the night.
The wind's feet could not take another step,
As tired as it was,
The wind could not say another word,
As one last drop of water fell from the sky,
And landed on the top of the sea, to settle down to sleep in
The dark coldness of the night.

1. Find five examples of personification. Circle them in red.

2. Which one is your favorite? _____

3. What words suggest the lightning is alive?_____

4. What went to sleep at the very end of the poem? _____

5. How do you know the wind was tired? _____

6. What poem line did you like best? _____

   Why?_____

7. What would you like to tell the poet about your response to her poem? _____

_____

Name _____

STRANGE DISAPPEARANCES

ADVENTURE #18 Take a trip to the Bermuda Triangle—if you dare! About 70 ships and airplanes have supposedly disappeared in this area of the Atlantic Ocean off the coast of Bermuda. Scientists are baffled. Do you want to try it?

Writers sometimes use figurative language to describe things like the Bermuda triangle. Similes and metaphors compare things which are not usually thought of as having anything in common. Read the similes and metaphors here. Then try writing some of your own!

Your room is the Bermuda Triangle.
Your room is a black hole,
(Things that go into it are never seen again!)
Kate Bridges, Gr.5

What's It Like?
by Laura Arndt, Gr.6

**Life is like a flower
      that is blooming.
The sky is like
      a never ending story,
Life is like a dark pool of water—
      You never know what's in it.**

Finish these:

My room is like _____.

Life is like _____.

My friend is like _____.

_____ is like _____.

_____ is as _____ as _____.

Life is Like
by Camille Morris, Gr.5

**Life is Like
A gift waiting to be opened
Counting to infinity and beyond
Walking somewhere you've never been
(You never know what's around the corner)
Unsolved mysteries
A never ending road (just keep on driving)
An everlasting gob-stopper**

Name _____

GOLDEN RECIPES

ADVENTURE #19

Search for gold with the forty-niners! Travel back to 1849 when the Gold Rush was in full swing in Northern California. Maybe you'll be one of the fortunate adventurers and end up with a pan full of golden nuggets!

Gus Grubb is the camp cook for the prospectors. He needs to get some supper ready fast, but his recipe directions are all out of order! Straighten them out for Gus by numbering the sentences in the correct order in each recipe.

GOLDEN NUGGET STEW

___Then cook them in hot chicken fat in a big kettle.
___First, cut up 5 chickens into small nuggets.
___Sprinkle with red pepper flakes before serving.
___Cook for 1 more hour.
___Roll the nuggets in flour mixed with salt and mustard powder.
___When the chicken is tender, throw in many handfuls of cut up carrots, turnips, onions, and potatoes.

HEARTY CORN BREAD

___Add 5 cups of whole wheat flour to the starter.
___Finally, stir in some chunks of cheese.
___Toss 1 cup of baking powder into the flour and cornmeal mixture.
___Next, mix in 5 cups of corn meal in with the flour and starter.
___Bake over a hot fire until it's brown on top.
___Start with ½ cup of sourdough starter.
___Sprinkle kernels of corn on top of the pan.
___Pour the mixture into a pan.

My number one secret ingredient is....

Catsup!

GREAT CAMPOUT GRUB

___Boil the hambone in 2 gallons of water for 3 hours.
___After the beans, add your favorite spices.
___Serve with hot corn bread.
___Start with a big old hambone.
___The second ingredient is 10 cans of beans— loads of fat, white beans.
___Cook for 1 hour over a hot camp fire.
___During the last 20 minutes of cooking, add 2 cups of sliced carrots.

Name

FIGHT THE FIERCEST BULL

ADVENTURE #20 We'll take you straight to Madrid for a bullfighting adventure. We supply the matador costume and the red cape. You supply the bravery!

These limericks about bullfighting are all mixed up. Number the lines in the right order so that each poem makes sense!

1.

____ By the creature's right horn,

____ A nervous matador named José

____ But the crowd just kept shouting, "Olé!"

____ Tried to outwit a bull yesterday.

____ His shoulder was torn

2.

____ And the people of Spain called him, "COOL"!

____ A bull had the name of Raoul

____ Anyone who would fight him was a fool.

____ His stomping was fearful,

____ And his snort was an earful.

4.

____ A man bought a bull in Madrid

____ In return for their adoring

____ So they traded him in for a squid!

____ As a pet for Alberto, his kid.

____ The bull got busy goring.

3.

____ As I did, I could hear the crowd roar.

____ And without thinking, I ran for the door!

____ And charged straight for my head.

____ Then the bull, he saw red.

____ I waved the cape, like a brave matador.

5.

____ "I can outsmart that old bull, no doubt!"

____ On a stretcher they carried her out.

____ But it sure was her worst!

____ The fight wasn't her first,

____ She said with an arrogant shout,

JOIN THE CIRCUS!

ADVENTURE #21 Running away with the circus is a popular fantasy. If you're not afraid of heights or tigers, this is just the right adventure for you!

When you walk the tightrope, which proverb will you remember?

HASTE MAKES WASTE.

NOTHING VENTURED, NOTHING GAINED!

HE WHO HESITATES IS LOST!

A proverb is a wise saying that teaches a lesson. Paraphrase these proverbs. (Rewrite them in your own words.)

1. Haste makes waste. _____

2. He who hesitates is lost! _____

3. Strike while the iron is hot. _____

4. A stitch in time saves nine. _____

5. Every cloud has a silver lining. _____

6. A rolling stone gathers no moss. _____

7. Nothing ventured, nothing gained! _____

8. Fish and visitors smell in three days. _____

9. Fools rush in where angels fear to tread. _____

10. Three may keep a secret if two are dead. _____

11. A bird in the hand is worth two in the bush! _____

12. Don't count your chickens before they hatch. _____

13. Don't change horses in the middle of a stream. _____

14. You can lead a horse to water, but you can't make him drink. _____

_____

Name

RIDE A RAGING RIVER

ADVENTURE #22 There's no thrill quite like a whitewater thrill! Travel to Costa Rica to take on some breathtaking rapids. If you know how to swim, we'll provide the wet suit and plenty of thrills—hopefully, with no spills!

An idiom is a kind of figurative speech. The words in an idiom mean something different from what they actually say. Paraphrase each of the idioms below. (Rewrite each idiom in your own words to explain what it really means.)

I got through the rapids by the skin of my teeth!

1. Are you pulling my leg? _____

2. She's going bananas. _____

3. We're in the doghouse now. _____

4. Has the cat got your tongue? _____

5. Will you please get off my back? _____

6. He's an old stick in the mud. _____

7. You'd better button your lip. _____

8. You've got me over a barrel. _____

9. I have a bone to pick with you! _____

10. It's a bad idea to rat on your friends. _____

11. Last night I slept like a log. _____

12. I went out on a limb for you. _____

13. She let the cat out of the bag. _____

14. She put her foot in her mouth again. _____

15. Time flies when you're having fun. _____

16. I thought the test was a piece of cake. _____

17. Well, that accident was the last straw. _____

18. These kids are driving me up a wall. _____

19. I passed the test by the skin of my teeth. _____

20. You could have knocked me over with a feather. _____

Name

MEET THE MAN OF LA MANCHA

ADVENTURE #23 Ride with the outlandish, mythical knight, Don Quixote, Man of la Mancha! See what fun he had on his outlandish adventures!

DRAGONS, WINDMILLS, & FIERCE ARMIES TO CONQUER

An unusual young man spent years reading wonderful tales about knighthood. His fantasies were filled with all the battles and quarrels, loves, adventures, dragons, and enchantments of the lives of knights. He read so much that his brain dried up and he got a little crazy. He decided to become a knight and do everything he had read about. He thought up an excellent, knightly name for himself: Don Quixote, Man of la Mancha.

The new knight got some old armor of his grandfather's and saddled up his weak old horse. He took Sancho, a simple neighbor, along as his squire. Off he went to have the adventures of a knight.

It's a four-armed giant!

Soon he came upon a gang of more than thirty giants. Sancho pointed out that these were windmills, not giants, but Don Quixote rode forward bravely to fight the giants, waving his sword wildly. He broke his sword and was thrown from his horse, but he still believed he had fought giants.

Next he saw two huge armies and decided to join one and lead it to defeat the other. The armies were two flocks of sheep, but Don Quixote did not seem to notice. Waving and whirling his sword, he charged into the midst of the sheep. The shepherds thought he was crazy. They threw stones at him to drive him off. He was sure he had been wounded by the swords of the enemy in battle.

Write a short summary of the story of Don Quixote.

_____

_____

_____

_____

_____

_____

Name

A LITTLE SLUGGISH

ADVENTURE #24 It may be the only slug race in the world. Would you want to miss it? Travel into the giant redwoods of California for one of the most unusual races you'll ever see. You get front row tickets. You can even race a slug, if you want to!

Morning Edition
Daily News

Valley Weather: Partly Cloudy

Vol. XXXIX No 14235 — Sunny Valley, California July 10, 1996 — 35¢

SLUG RACES COMING TO AREA SOON

There's more wildlife to watch and enjoy next month in the Pacific Coast redwoods of Northern California.

Visitors flock to Prairie Creek Redwoods State Park on the Pacific Ocean for many reasons. After they play in the ocean, they can watch elk, bears, bobcats, and foxes, which are plentiful in the ancient forest park. Campers can park trailers and hike the beautiful trails through the canyons to the ocean.

But next month, there will be another fascinating reason to visit the park. On August 16, the 29th annual Banana Slug Derby will be held. A variety of races will be held and prizes will be awarded to winning slugs in several categories.

One of last year's top winning banana slugs poses with her owner and her trophy. Over seven hundred spectators watched the races last year.

Two hundred trophies made by locals will be given. There will be food and fun for everyone.

Visitors are invited to attend the derby. "You can bring your own slug, or we'll loan you one from our slugarium at the visitor's center," says Park Ranger Robert Roberts. Park rangers have already started hunting for speedy slugs. Visitors need to know, however, that this is a very competitive race. Therefore, any slugs brought in from the outside will be given a slug drug test before they are eligible to take part in the races.

For information about the Banana Slug Derby, call the Prairie Creek Park Visitor's Center at 707-488-2171.

Answer the questions T (True) or F (False) based on your reading of the article.

_____ 1. Visitors come to the park only for the slug races.
_____ 2. The park is a beautiful place to stay.
_____ 3. Camping is permitted in the park.
_____ 4. The Banana Slug Derby is a lot of fun.
_____ 5. No one would want to look at slugs.
_____ 6. The derby is a new idea.
_____ 7. Everyone who races a slug brings it along from home.
_____ 8. The local people support the idea of the derby.
_____ 9. Park rangers do not allow anyone to touch the slugs that live in the park.
_____ 10. What would you conclude about a slug that was disqualified from the race?

_____

Name

YOUR NAME IN NEON!

ADVENTURE #25 Take a trip with us down to the home of country music, Nashville, Tennessee. Live your dream of performing at the Grand Ole Opry! Maybe you'll even become a star!

Read these pieces of writing about Nashville and neon! Then tell the author's purpose and point of view for each one.

1. How exciting to see Talula's name in lights! She's been a'singin' her heart out since she was just an itsy, bitsy girl. I watched her make a pretend microphone from her mama's egg beater when she was just knee-high to a dinner table. She just stood there and belted out the tune "Your Cheatin' Heart" at the top of her little lungs. If anyone deserves to be a big star—it's Talula.

Who's writing? Circle one.
   a. a character in the story
   b. a narrator who is not in the story
   c. a narrator who is a character in the story
What is the author's purpose in writing this?

_____

2. I headed for Nashville at age 16 with my guitar over my shoulder and a song in my head. I planned to be a star. Ten years later, without a dollar to my name and no hit songs, I headed out of town. Everyone in Nashville wants to be a star. I heard, "No thanks," a thousand times. No one wanted my singin', my song writin', or my guitar playin'. This is a town that'll break your heart and your bank account.

Who's writing? Circle one.
   a. a character in the story
   b. a narrator who is not in the story
   c. a narrator who is a character in the story
What is the author's purpose in writing this?

_____

NEWS FLASH!!

3. Rising Star James T. Twang has a new hit. His song, "You've Broken My Fax, My Computer, and My Heart" leaped to the top of the Country Music Charts last week. This is good news for a hometown boy.

Who's writing? Circle one.
   a. a character in the story
   b. a narrator who is not in the story
   c. a narrator who is a character in the story
What is the author's purpose in writing this?

_____

IT'S A GAS!

4. Every time you see those brilliant colored lights, you'll know that they are made with gas. A French scientist, Georges Claude, figured out how to take rare gases out of the atmosphere and put them into tubes. An electric spark is sent streaking through the tubes. Different gases give off different colors as the spark goes through them, so different gases are put in the tubes to create different colors. Other colors are made by using tubes that are tinted or coated with certain powders that give off a colored glow. When someone's name lights up in neon, this is how it happens!

Who's writing? Circle one.
   a. a character in the story
   b. a narrator who is not in the story
   c. a narrator who is a character in the story
What is the author's purpose in writing this?

_____

Name _____

ALONE IN THE TANGLED WOODS

ADVENTURE #26 This is the ultimate solo camping experience. We'll pack some basic supplies and drop you off in a deep, tangled forest. You can enjoy the solitude while you test your endurance. Who knows, maybe you won't really be alone out there!

Something's Coming
by Kathryn Harriss, Gr. 5

Something's coming!
Coming, coming closer!
Closer, closer still!
It walks, it talks, it stalks in the night.
Feel its breath upon your face.
Shield your eyes from its brilliant glow.
Something's coming!
Coming, coming closer!
What is it?
Who knows?

Tell what you think . . .

1. What is coming?

_____

2. What will happen next?

_____

_____

3. What was the author's purpose as she wrote this?

_____

_____

4. What line or phrase is most effective?

_____

_____

Tell what you think . . .

5. What is the place that is far from civilization?

_____

6. What are the clues?

_____

7. What was the author's purpose as she wrote this?

_____

8. What line or phrase is most effective?

_____

Far From Civilization
by Linda NewComb, Gr. 5

I know I am far from civilization
When I hear the fish jumping
The rain hitting the tent
And
Rocks falling
When I feel the cool chill in the air
When I see the top of my west wind
Tent
And
When I smell the sweet scent of
White bark pines
And
Fresh air.
That is how I know I am
Far from civilization.

Name _____

TRACKING DOWN CLUES

ADVENTURE #27 Track down clues and crimes with the world's most famous detective, Sherlock Holmes.

You can snoop around Sherlock's Detective Log and see what cases he's working on. After you read the notes on each page, you can write your prediction to help solve the case.

Case #1 *Mrs. McCurty's Missing Jewels*
Jewels are stolen at 8 P.M. Friday from dresser drawer.
Suspects:
> **Nanny Opal:** did not come to work Saturday
>> Her sister and doctor say she is sick.
> **Grandma Ruby:** stays locked in her room
>> She has taken the jewels before.
> **The Butler:** has bulging pockets
>> He is angry at his employer for refusing a pay raise.
> **Neighbor, Professor Gem:** recently put a large sum into his bank account
>> He is really Simon Topaz, previously arrested for jewel theft.

Predict: Who will be arrested? _____

Why do you think so? _____

Case #2 *The Missing Raw Meat*
Butcher reports 22 pounds raw meat missing, Saturday midnight.
Suspects:
> **Count Janson's cat:** has an extended belly
> **Brewster's dog:** has stolen meat several times before
>> has a satisfied look on his face on Sunday, raw meat on his paws
> **Cook at la Mancha Hotel:** served beef rolls Sunday,
>> was out of town until Sunday morning at 6 A.M.
> **Garbage Collector:** seen digging through Butcher's trash

Predict: Who will be arrested? _____

Why do you think so? _____

Case #3 *Broken Lamppost on Canterbury Lane*
- Yellow paint found on bent lamppost Wednesday night; broken glass on ground from burst lamp
- Talked to all homeowners in the area
- Checked all carriage repair shops
- Checked with shops selling yellow paint
- Found names of owners of 7 yellow carriages

What should Sherlock do next? _____

_____

Name

RACE WITH THE DOGS

ADVENTURE #28 Bring your warmest clothes to Alaska, because you'll be driving a team of racing sled dogs over a snow-covered course! You might even get good enough to join the toughest race of all: the Iditarod International Sled Dog Race.

Read the weather reports for several days of the Iditarod. Then use your judgment to make the predictions and draw the conclusions asked for below.

DAY 1: WEATHER REPORT
The skies will be clear today, with temperatures at 0°. Light, fluffy snow covers the ground.

DAY 2: WEATHER REPORT
Temperatures are warming. Expect a light rain, which will turn to freezing rain this afternoon.

DAY 3: WEATHER REPORT
Heavy fog will move in, bringing moist, wet air hovering over the snow. Winds will be harsh this evening.

DAY 4: WEATHER REPORT
Extreme blizzard conditions are reported today. Warnings are out for complete white-out conditions. Winds are blowing at 60 mph with drifts up to six feet.

DAY 5: WEATHER REPORT
Today the temperatures will climb to 20° with light snow showers and light winds.

DAY 6: WEATHER REPORT
Temperatures have taken a plunge. At noon, we recorded –25° with a –80° wind chill factor. Everyone is warned to stay indoors. It is extremely dangerous for people or animals to be outdoors in these conditions.

What do you think?

_____ 1. On what day might the racers have the best conditions?

_____ 2. If ice is a problem, what day(s) might give the racers problems?

_____ 3. What troubles might the drivers and dogs have on Day 4?

_____ 4. What troubles might they have on Day 3?

_____ 5. What kind of progress do you think they'll make on Day 5?

_____ 6. What do you think the racing teams will do on Day 6?

Name _____

THE THRILL OF A BIG WAVE

ADVENTURE #29 Grab some sunscreen and your surfboard. We'll take you to Hawaii, Australia, South Africa, and South America in search of the biggest waves in the world! Travel up to 35 miles per hour on top of a wave. Insurance is included!

Read the statements about the surfers. Then answer the questions below.

Jeri wears glasses.

Jules is from Malibu.

Jess is not from Big Sur.

Jo is not from Mexico.

Jo is not from Big Sur.

Jo wears stripes when surfing.

Jamie is not from Australia.

The surfer from Maui is male.

The oldest surfer is from Malibu.

The surfer from Mexico wears glasses.

The surfer from Australia has curly hair.

Jess always wears a life vest when surfing.

_____ 1. Which surfer lives in Big Sur?

_____ 2. Which surfer is from Australia?

_____ 3. Which surfer is from Mexico?

_____ 4. Which surfer is from Maui?

_____ 5. Which surfer wears a polka-dotted suit?

Name

A STOMACH DROPPER

ADVENTURE #30 Be the first person to ride the Heartstopper, the world's newest and biggest and most terrifying roller coaster. Don't choose this adventure unless you have a stomach of iron!

THIRTEEN THRILLS on THIRTEEN HILLS

You have waited in line for two hours to ride the new upside-down, triple loop, heart-stopping rollercoaster. It has thirteen awesome hills. While you wait, you begin to imagine the screams and screeches you'll soon be hearing.

You are nervous, excited, impatient to get on. You trust this rollercoaster, or you wouldn't be trying it out. Even though you're the first customer to ride, you are sure it will be safe. When it's time to ride, you don't care how it works. You just want to get on!

A moving chain will pull the car to the top. When the car gets to the peak of the hill and starts to curve over, gravity pulls it down the steep incline. At the very top of each hill, your body keeps going up out of your seat because of inertia. You feel like you are flying, but soon the gravity has you back in your seat again. At every curve and every upside-down loop, centripetal force pushes you against your seat. This is why you don't fall out. Finally, friction slows down the coaster and stops it.

The ride is over. You enjoyed every minute of it. Your stomach feels great, and you want to ride again right away!

1. The author makes some assumptions about the way the rider feels or will feel. Underline these with a red pen or marker.

2. What do you think of the writer's approach of telling the reader how he or she will feel about the ride? _____

   _____

3. Did the writer have good reasons to claim that the rider enjoyed the ride? _____

4. Evaluate how well the writer explained the workings of the roller coaster. _____

   _____

   _____

   _____

Name

HERE COMES THE JUDGE

ADVENTURE #31 Just what you've always wanted! This week, **you** get to be the judge. Take over Judge Weary's courtroom, and decide the cases yourself. The black robe and gavel will be provided.

Read the facts you have been provided for each case. Then write your judgment. Tell what you will order to settle the question.

CASE #1 *The Deceased Cat*
Miss LaGrady claims that her neighbor killed her cat. She found the cat dead on her doorstep, with traces of slimy green bologna on its whiskers and paws. Remains of the same bologna were found in the garbage can of her next door neighbor, Mr. Clam. Should Mr. Clam pay for the cat's burial and Miss LaGrady's grief counseling?

Your judgment _____

CASE #2 *Neighbors vs The Magenta Family*
The entire neighborhood association is suing the Magenta Family for disrupting the neighborhood. They claim that the purple spots that the Magentas painted on their house are an eyesore. They say the awful color drives home buyers away. They have asked that the Magentas be forced to repaint their house and pay each neighbor a sum of $1000.

Your judgment _____

CASE #3 *The Potato Chip Deceit*
Mr. Port claims that the Crunchy Potato Chip Company is responsible for his gain of 100 pounds. He points out that the potato chip bag says that the chips contain 200 calories. He thought that meant 200 calories per bag, so he ate a bag every day for two years. When he gained so much weight, he became suspicious of the chips and had them analyzed. The truth is, the chips contain 200 calories per serving. That adds up to 2000 per bag. Should the company pay Mr. Port $3000 to go to a weight loss program?

Your judgment _____

Name _____

BRING A MASK

ADVENTURE #32 Find yourself a great costume and a wonderful mask. You're invited to be the guest of King Louis XIV at the great palace of Versailles!

Read about each guest at the ball. Then write a question you would ask that character in order to find out more about her or him.

Count Pompous is strutting about the great hall with a fancy hat and his high-heeled boots. He will probably keep his nose in the air the entire evening.

Countess Dainté dances lightly across the ballroom floor. She seems to float around the room with a light step. Everything about her seems soft, sweet, and sincere.

Lady Columbine is busy showing off her beauty and grace. She just knows that everyone is looking at her, and no one else. If you are not a young, handsome, wealthy prince, she won't want to waste her time on you!

What a jolly fellow is the friendly Jacques Joli! It's a pleasure to have his company. He has a clever, happy word for every guest.

Little Prince Mischief just loves these parties, too! He is so small, that guests hardly notice him. He lurks around under tables and behind curtains, having loads of fun!

There's Dowager La-de-da! How honored you should be to come into the presence of this rich old dame. Be sure you do not say anything rowdy or improper in her presence. She has no time for foolishness.

Judge d'Éclaire is a very important man. He loves these parties because of the plentiful food. Oh, how he loves to eat! If you stop to visit with him, do bring him a pastry or two.

Name

43 *Basic Skills/Reading Comprehension 4-5*

THE WORLD'S LUXURY TRAIN

ADVENTURE #33 It's the train of mystery and luxury! Ride the famous Orient Express from Paris to Istanbul. You will need to pack lightly. There's not much room for luggage in your sleeper compartment.

Read about the mysterious happenings on the Orient Express on the next page (page 45). Then write five to ten words that you think would describe each character.

The Porter _____

Countess L'Orange _____

Dr. Plumper _____

The Mystery Man _____

Madeline Merry _____

Mrs. Mergatroid Matisse _____

Oliver Snooze _____

The Burglar _____

Use with page 45.

Name

SOMETHING IS STRANGE ON THE ORIENT EXPRESS

At first it seems like an ordinary train trip, but then, no trip on the Orient Express is ever really ordinary! This train has such a history of luxury and mystery that you can almost smell strange happenings in the air!

Madeline Merry wanders around to explore the train. This is her first trip on the Orient Express. She looks like an innocent child playing in the aisles, yet she loves to play detective. She is really out snooping. As she passes the countess, she notices that the little dog has a small packet hidden beneath his neck. Her watchful eye does not miss the countess slipping something into the doctor's open bag as she squeezes past him in the aisle. Next, she knows that the man in the berth is snoring, but why are his eyes peeking out from beneath mostly-closed lids? He does not seem to care that a sneaky fellow is reaching out for his watch.

Madeline plays with her yo-yo, but her ears do not miss the whispering behind a closed curtain. Nor can she ignore the large lump in the pocket of the proper-looking Mrs. Matisse. Why is Mrs. Matisse hovering awfully close to the mysterious man who hides behind his collar? And what is in the package she is guarding so closely?

As Madeline roams along the aisle, the train suddenly jerks to a stop. Baggage and people fly everywhere, and then the lights go out. There is much squealing and screaming in the dark. When the lights are turned back on, the woman who claims to be a countess is screeching, "My doggie! My doggie! Someone has taken my doggie!" As passengers are scurrying around, Madeline sees that the doctor's bag is on the shelf and another bag is in his hand. Mrs. Matisse has lost her hat, and the porter is missing. Just then, Madeline's mother comes and grabs her by the hand. It is time for her family to leave the train.

Write a short explanation for each element of the story.

Story Theme	
Characters	
Setting	
Plot	
Point of View (Who is telling the story?)	

Use with page 44.

Name

AN ANCIENT ART

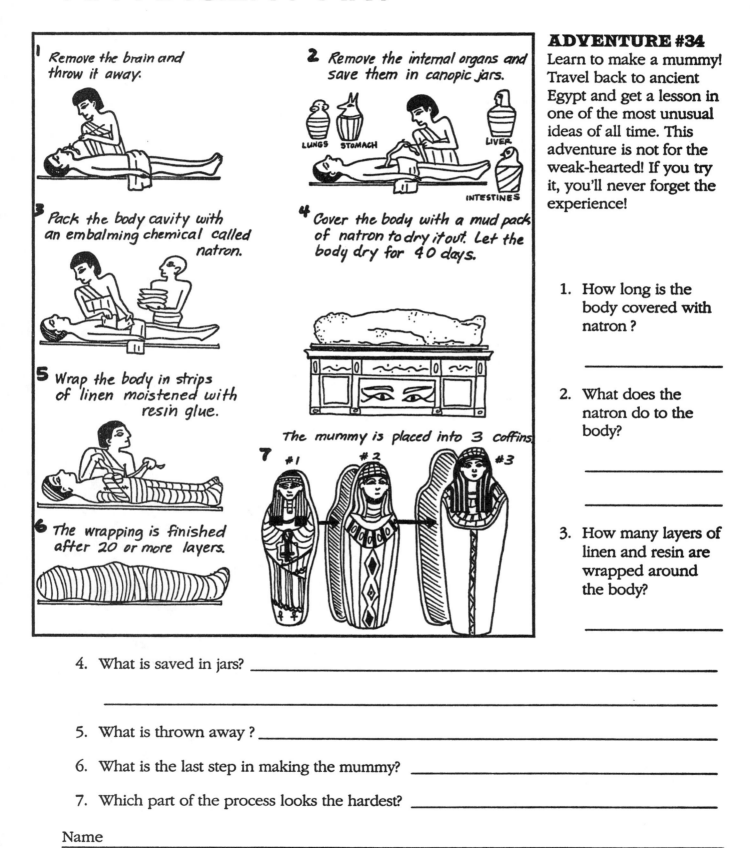

1 Remove the brain and throw it away.

2 Remove the internal organs and save them in canopic jars.

LUNGS STOMACH LIVER INTESTINES

3 Pack the body cavity with an embalming chemical called natron.

4 Cover the body with a mud pack of natron to dry it out. Let the body dry for 40 days.

5 Wrap the body in strips of linen moistened with resin glue.

6 The wrapping is finished after 20 or more layers.

The mummy is placed into 3 coffins

7 #1 #2 #3

ADVENTURE #34
Learn to make a mummy! Travel back to ancient Egypt and get a lesson in one of the most unusual ideas of all time. This adventure is not for the weak-hearted! If you try it, you'll never forget the experience!

1. How long is the body covered with natron ?

_____

2. What does the natron do to the body?

_____

_____

3. How many layers of linen and resin are wrapped around the body?

_____

4. What is saved in jars? _____

_____

5. What is thrown away ? _____

6. What is the last step in making the mummy? _____

7. Which part of the process looks the hardest? _____

Name _____

46

WELCOME TO CAMELOT

ADVENTURE #35 Meet King Arthur! Visit Camelot! Get your very own suit of mail! Learn to fight a dragon, if you wish! Many have dreamed of this adventure. You can actually live it!

Sir Prance-a-lot is caught in the depths of a terrible dungeon, fighting a fire-breathing dragon. The dragon has wrapped itself around the knight, and it seems he will have no chance of escape. Sir Prance-a-lot is a brave and skilled warrior, so perhaps he will defeat this wingless dragon yet!

Meanwhile, back inside the castle, a worried damsel is chained to a pillar. She is waiting for Sir Prance-a-lot to slay the dragon and rescue her. She does not have to wait long! Here comes the dashing knight to the rescue! How fortunate she is to have such a brave friend to save her from peril.

What is wrong with this story? Rewrite the story, using correct information supplied by the picture.

_____

_____

_____

_____

_____

_____

_____

Name

DROP INTO THE ALPS

ADVENTURE #36 There's nothing quite like a helicopter adventure!
Bring your skis, and we'll supply the rest. We will drop you into the Swiss
Alps for the most extraordinary ski experience of your life!

Swiss SkiDrop, Inc.
HELICOPTER SCHEDULE

DEPARTURE CITY	Destination	Departure Days	Return Days
ZURICH	Drop 1	Tues, Thurs	Fri, Sun
	Drop 2	Wed, Sat	Mon, Thurs
	Drop 3	Sun, Wed	Tues, Fri
BASEL	Drop 1	Wed, Sat	Sun, Wed
	Drop 2	Sun, Wed	Tues, Fri
	Drop 3	Thurs, Sun	Sat, Tues
BERN	Drop 1	Fri, Tues	Mon, Fri
	Drop 2	Wed, Tues	Sun, Fri
	Drop 3	Sat, Wed	Tues, Fri
LAUSANNE	Drop 1	Mon, Fri	Wed, Sun
	Drop 2	Thurs, Tues	Mon, Thurs
	Drop 3	Sun, Tues	Wed, Sat
CHUR	Drop 1	Thurs	Mon
	Drop 2	Mon	Fri

Use the information on the table to answer the questions.

1. Leaving from Basel, can you fly to Drop 1 and stay for only 3 days (including travel days)? _____

2. If you wanted to head for Drop 2 on a Wednesday, what cities could you depart from?
   _____

3. Where can you go on Tuesday from Lausanne? _____

4. Can you fly to Drop 3 from Chur? _____

5. What days can you return to Bern from Drop 3? _____

6. Can you return to Zurich from Drop 2 on Tuesday? _____

7. If you want to leave Zurich on Wednesday and return the following Monday, which ski area
   must you choose to be dropped in? _____

8. Can you fly to Drop 1 from Chur on Monday? _____

9. How many choices for departure are there on Friday? _____

10. How many choices for returns are there on Sunday? _____

Name

A RIDE WITH "THE KING"

Most Expensive Items of Rock Stars' Belongings Sold at Auctions

Item	Year of Sale	Price
John Lennon's 1965 Rolls-Royce Phantom V touring limousine	1985	$ 2,299,000
Jimi Hendrix's Fender Stratocaster electric guitar	1990	$ 370,260
An acoustic guitar that had been owned by George Michael, Paul McCartney, and David Bowie	1994	$ 341,000
Buddy Holly's Gibson electric guitar	1990	$ 242,000
John Lennon's 1970 Mercedes-Benz 600 limousine	1989	$ 213,125
Elvis Presley's 1942 Martin D-18 guitar	1991	$ 180,000
Elvis Presley's 1960 Rolls-Royce Phantom V touring limousine	1986	$ 162,800
Charlie Parker's Grafton saxophone	1991	$ 144,925
John Lennon's recording of his singing at a 1957 church fair	1994	$ 121,675
Buddy Holly's Fender Stratocaster electric guitar	1990	$ 110,000

ADVENTURE #37 This one will take a bit of time travel. We'll take you back to the 1960s for a ride in the Rolls Royce. A lot of Elvis fans will be jealous of you!

Use the information from the chart to answer the questions below.

_____ 1. How many cars are listed?

_____ 2. How many guitars are listed?

_____ 3. How many musical instruments are included that are not guitars?

_____ 4. What was the highest price brought by an item in 1994?

_____ 5. What was the highest price brought by an item in 1990?

_____ 6. Which sold for more money: Elvis's guitar or his car?

_____ 7. Which sold for more money: John Lennon's car or recording?

_____ 8. How much more was paid for Buddy Holly's Gibson guitar than the Fender guitar?

_____ 9. How many items were sold from 1985 to 1990?

_____ 10. How much was spent for the items sold in 1990?

Name _____

HIGH CLIMBER

ADVENTURE #38 You've watched others do it—now try it yourself. Start your building-climbing adventure with the Empire State Building. If you like it, you can go on to try more of the world's tallest buildings.

Use the information on the graph to answer the questions.

THE WORLD'S TALLEST BUILDINGS

Building	height in feet 1,000	1,050	1,100	1,150	1,200	1,250	1,300	1,350	1,400	1,450	1,500
Amoco Building Chicago											
Sears Tower Chicago											
World Trade Center New York											
Petronas Towers Malaysia											
Baiyoke II Tower Thailand											
T & C Tower Taiwan											
Shun Hing Square China											
John Hancock Center Chicago											
Empire State Building New York											
Sky Central Plaza China											

1. Which building is 1,082 feet tall? _____

2. What is the tallest building shown? _____

3. What is the shortest building shown? _____

4. Which two buildings are closest in height? _____

5. Which building is 1,250 feet tall? _____

6. Which building is 1,368 feet tall? _____

7. Which building is 1,127 feet tall? _____

8. Which building is almost 200 feet higher than the Sky Central Plaza? _____

9. Which building is about 100 feet shorter than the T & C Tower? _____

10. Which building is about 30 feet taller than the Sears Tower? _____

Name _____

IT'S GREAT TO BE QUEEN

ADVENTURE #39 Hop aboard the time machine and travel all the way back to A.D. 593 and visit with the world's 10 longest-reigning queens along the way. Spend a day sharing a throne with each one. Bring dressy clothes. We'll loan you a crown!

Follow the directions below to complete the graph.

	Reign, in Years 30 35 40 45 50 55 60 65 70
WORLD'S LONGEST-REIGNING QUEENS	**QUEEN**

Write each queen's name on the graph as you read about her. Color a bar to show how long she reigned.

1. Queen Isabella II of Spain reigned from 1833 to 1868.

2. Queen Maria Theresa of Hungary reigned from 1740 to 1780.

3. Queen Wu Chao of China reigned from 655 to 705.

4. Queen Victoria of the United Kingdom reigned from 1837 to 1901.

5. Queen Salote Tubou of Tonga reigned from 1918 to 1965.

6. Queen Suiko Tenno of Japan reigned from 593 to 628.

7. Queen Elizabeth I of the United Kingdom reigned from 1558 to 1603.

8. Queen Elizabeth II of the United Kingdom still reigns. Her reign began in 1952.

9. Queen Joanna I of Italy reigned from 1343 to 1381.

10. Queen Maria I of Portugal reigned from 1777 to 1816.

11. Queen Wilhelmina of the Netherlands reigned from 1890 to 1948.

Name

A SWEET RECORD

ADVENTURE #40 Get yourself in the *Guinness Book of World Records*—with a little help from our company. We'll teach you the secret tricks to help you eat the largest ice cream sundae of all time. You like ice cream, we hope!

Follow the directions below to draw the sundae. You'll need markers or crayons.

1. Draw seven large scoops of bubble gum–raisin ice cream on the bottom layer.
2. Draw eight long slices of banana around the edges of this layer.
3. Draw six large scoops of peppermint-fudge ice cream on the next layer.
4. Draw five large scoops of lemon chiffon sherbet on the next layer.
5. Draw a layer of crushed chocolate cookies on top of the lemon sherbet.
6. Draw four large scoops of blueberry-marshmallow ice cream on the next layer.
7. Draw strawberry sauce on top of this layer.
8. Draw three huge scoops of pumpkin pie ice cream on the next layer.
9. Draw caramel sauce on top of this layer.
10. Draw two huge scoops of chocolate chunk ice cream on top of this.
11. Draw sticky hot fudge running all over the sundae.
12. Draw fluffy squirts of whipped cream all over the sundae.
13. Draw loads of nuts sprinkled on the sundae.
14. Draw one huge cherry on the top.

Name

THE GREATEST COWBOY

ADVENTURE #41 Join the wild escapades of the great cowboy hero,
Pecos Bill! Ride a cyclone, tame rattlesnakes, and learn to lasso a speeding train!

A TALL COWBOY TALE

Pecos Bill was the greatest cowboy of all—a hero to all cowboys. When he was a baby, he fell out of his family's wagon and was left behind along the Pecos River. A family of coyotes adopted him, and he thought he was a coyote for many years.

Some cowboys found him and took him in. They taught him cowboy skills. He grew to be so big and strong and brave, that he could do far more than the other cowboys.

Bill was eight feet tall and carried seven guns and nine knives in his belt. He could ride the biggest, most powerful horses. No horse could throw him. He could ride anything—no matter how wild. One time he rode a mountain lion, using a rattlesnake as a whip. Another time, he rode a wild cyclone!

One day, two rattlesnakes bothered Bill. He grabbed one in each hand and shook the daylights out of them. Then he tied their tails together and hung them in a tree.

Pecos Bill could lasso whole herds of cattle at one time. He could lasso anything! The best trick he ever did happened the day he spied a runaway train. Bill just grabbed his lasso, and lassoed that train!

Yes, Pecos Bill is still talked about in cowboy country. If you go to the Arizona desert, you will still see the footprints that his huge horses left among the rocks.

1. What do you think is true about Pecos Bill?

   _____

   _____

   _____

2. Underline phrases or statements that you think might be exaggerated.

3. What other great feats or tricks would you like to see Pecos Bill do?

   _____

   _____

   _____

   _____

   _____

   _____

Name _____

HUNTING FOR NESSIE

ADVENTURE #42 You have wondered if it's real! Board a boat on a cold dark Scottish lake, and search through the fog for the Loch Ness monster yourself.

TERROR IN SCOTLAND

I've seen the fierce winged dragon
With mouth of flame and smoke,
And dreamed of the elusive Sasquatch
Still chasing me when I awoke.

I've ridden the great Greek Satyr
With body part man, part beast.
Done battle with the monstrous Hydra
Who wore nine heads, at least!

I've flown on the grotesque Griffin
Eagle head, lion body and tail.
Come face to face with a Yeti,
And shuddered till I grew pale.

I've danced with a mighty Unicorn
(Now does that sound absurd?)
Escaped from a deadly Siren,
A creature half woman, half bird.

But I've never shrieked in horror,
Never trembled and shook with dread.
I have never cried like a baby,
Nor stopped breathing like the dead.
No, I never knew sheer terror,
Not awake or asleep, I confess...
Until I saw, for a moment
The Monster of Loch Ness...
The massive
rising
grasping
writhing
SERPENT
of
Loch
Ness.

1. Which creature in the poem would you least like to meet? _____

2. Which line in the poem gives the best description of a creature? _____
_____
_____

3. Tell why the title is a good one. (Or, tell why it is not.) _____
_____
_____
_____
_____

4. What are some of the most effective words the poet used? _____
_____
_____

5. Write a one-sentence summary of the poem. _____
_____
_____

Name _____

APPENDIX

CONTENTS

LITERARY DEVICES

Writers use literary devices to make writing interesting!

alliteration — repeated consonant sounds in a phrase or sentence.

Alliteration usually occurs at the beginning of words (*wee Willie Winkie*). Alliteration sets a rhythm or mood to sentences and phrases. It is fun and pleasing to the ear.

characterization — the techniques a writer uses to let the reader know about the characters. This allows readers to know about a character's personality, appearance, or behavior.

figurative language — a way of using language that expands the literal meaning of the words and gives a new or more interesting twist to the words.

hyperbole — extreme exaggeration used to increase the effect of a statement. (*I've asked you a million times to clean your room.*)

imagery — details that appeal to the senses. (*Sweet, slow drops of deep purple juice drip from the corners of my mouth and flow in little blueberry rivers down to my chin.*)

metaphor — a comparison between two things that are not ordinarily alike. (*My little brother is a tornado.*)

mood — the feeling in a piece of writing. Mood is set by a combination of the words and sounds used, the setting, the imagery, and the details. Mood may give a feeling of mystery, rush, softness, cold, fear, darkness, etc.

onomatopoeia — a use of a word that makes the same sound as its meaning or as what it does (*swish, crackle, zip*).

personification — giving human characteristics to a nonliving object. (*Lightning grabbed for me.*)

plot — a series of events that the writer uses to make a story. The plot usually contains a telling of a situation or problem, the development of the situation, and a final resolving of the problem or situation.

point of view — tells who is telling the story. The story may be told by a character in the story, a narrator who is in the story, or a narrator who is not in the story.

rhyme — repeating of sounds. Rhymes may occur at the end of lines (*one, two, buckle my shoe*) or within the lines (*we went sliding and gliding, hiding and flying across the slippery ice*).

setting — the place where a story occurs.

simile — a comparison between two unlike things using the word *like* or *as* to connect the two. (*Losing a friend is **like** peanut butter and jelly apart. July moves **as** slowly **as** a sleepy snail.*)

theme — the main meaning or idea of a piece of writing. It includes the topic and a viewpoint or opinion about the topic.

tone — the approach a writer takes toward the topic. The tone may be playful, hostile, humorous, serious, argumentative, etc.

READING COMPREHENSION
SKILLS TEST

Each correct answer is worth 1 point.
Total possible points: 60
Give a title to each article.

1. _____

   The largest painting ever done by one artist is *The Battle of Gettysburg*. Paul Pilippoteaux finished it in 1883. It's about as big as a football field. No wonder it took over two years to paint!

2. _____

   Wolfgang Amadeus Mozart started composing music at age four. Even though he died at the young age of 35, he wrote 1000 pieces of music in his lifetime.

3. _____

   The largest supply of sunken treasure in the world lies on the bottom of the Atlantic Ocean off the coast of the Bahamas. There are about 2000 Spanish galleons that sank in the 16th century.

4. _____

   The Spanish painter, Picasso, is history's most productive painter. He painted over 13,000 paintings. In addition, he did many sculptures, book illustrations, and engravings in his 91 years of life.

5. _____

   The largest cake ever baked weighed 58 tons. It was baked to celebrate the 100th birthday of a town in Alabama.

6. What do all the articles have in common?

   _____

   _____

GREAT DANCE RECORDS

KIND of RECORD	The Dance or Dancers	Date	Number or length
Largest Dance Occasion	Moonlight Serenade Dance Buffalo, NY	1984	25,000 people
Largest Single Dance (everyone dancing at once)	Square Dance Louisville, KY	1983	20,000 dancers
Longest Dance Line	The Super Conga Dance Miami, FL	1988	119,986 dancers in a line
Longest Dancing Dragon	School children in Great Britain	1989	985 feet long
Most Exhausting Dance	Mike Ritof & Edith Boudreaux Chicago, IL	1930-1931	5,148 hours, 28 ½ minutes
Lowest Height Limbo Stick Anyone Danced Under	Dennis Walston Kent, WA	1991	6 inches from floor

7. Which record was set outside of the USA? _____

8. Which record was set by one person?

   _____

9. Which record included the most people?

   _____

10. Which record took longest?

    _____

11. What year was the limbo record set?

    _____

12. What state was the site of the Super Conga Dance? _____

13. Which record surprises you most?

    _____

14. Why? _____

    _____

    _____

Name _____

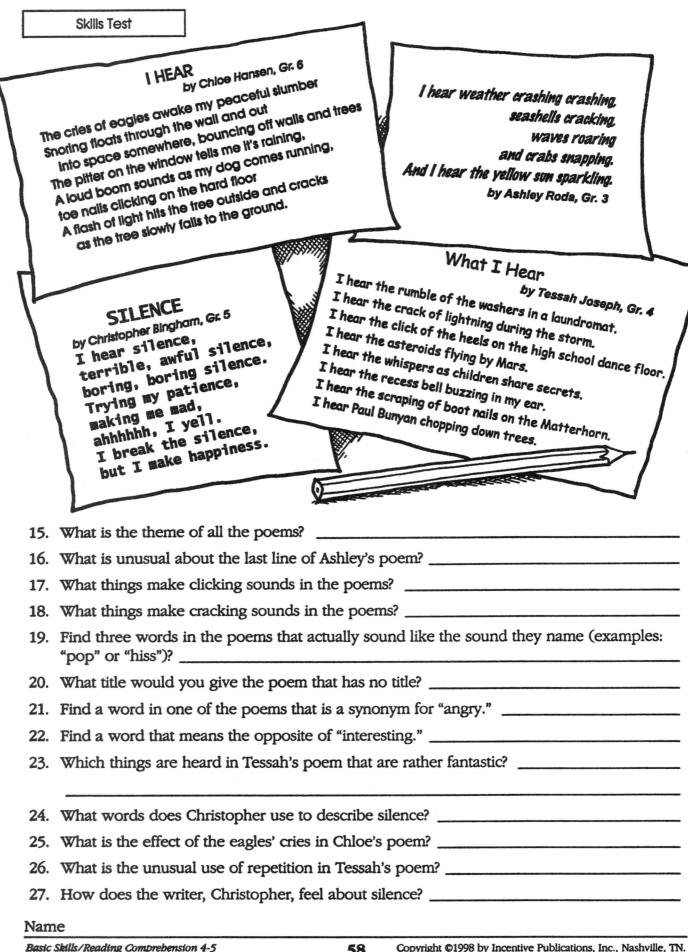

I HEAR
by Chloe Hansen, Gr. 6

The cries of eagles awake my peaceful slumber
Snoring floats through the wall and out
Into space somewhere, bouncing off walls and trees
The pitter on the window tells me it's raining.
A loud boom sounds as my dog comes running,
toe nails clicking on the hard floor
A flash of light hits the tree outside and cracks
as the tree slowly falls to the ground.

I hear weather crashing crashing,
seashells cracking,
waves roaring
and crabs snapping.
And I hear the yellow sun sparkling.
by Ashley Roda, Gr. 3

SILENCE
by Christopher Bingham, Gr. 5
I hear silence,
terrible, awful silence,
boring, boring silence.
Trying my patience,
making me mad,
ahhhhhh, I yell.
I break the silence,
but I make happiness.

What I Hear
by Tessah Joseph, Gr. 4
I hear the rumble of the washers in a laundromat.
I hear the crack of lightning during the storm.
I hear the click of the heels on the high school dance floor.
I hear the asteroids flying by Mars.
I hear the whispers as children share secrets.
I hear the recess bell buzzing in my ear.
I hear the scraping of boot nails on the Matterhorn.
I hear Paul Bunyan chopping down trees.

15. What is the theme of all the poems? _____

16. What is unusual about the last line of Ashley's poem? _____

17. What things make clicking sounds in the poems? _____

18. What things make cracking sounds in the poems? _____

19. Find three words in the poems that actually sound like the sound they name (examples: "pop" or "hiss")? _____

20. What title would you give the poem that has no title? _____

21. Find a word in one of the poems that is a synonym for "angry." _____

22. Find a word that means the opposite of "interesting." _____

23. Which things are heard in Tessah's poem that are rather fantastic? _____
_____

24. What words does Christopher use to describe silence? _____

25. What is the effect of the eagles' cries in Chloe's poem? _____

26. What is the unusual use of repetition in Tessah's poem? _____

27. How does the writer, Christopher, feel about silence? _____

Name _____

Read the poem and the sentences below. Next to each one, write the code letters of the literary devices that have been used. There may be more than one.

P = personification	**I** = Idiom	**M** = metaphor
A = alliteration	**S** = simile	**E** = exaggeration

_____ 28. Read the poem *The Wind* and and write the code letters.

_____ 29. *The queen is quite quick at quilting!*

_____ 30. *You are driving me up a wall with your constant complaining!*

_____ 31. **Today the clouds are dragons breathing fires of stinging raindrops.**

_____ 32. A sneaky fog stretched out its long, silvery fingers, reaching for me.

_____ 33. My calculator is like an annoying little brother.

_____ 34. **It was so hot that the chickens laid scrambled eggs.**

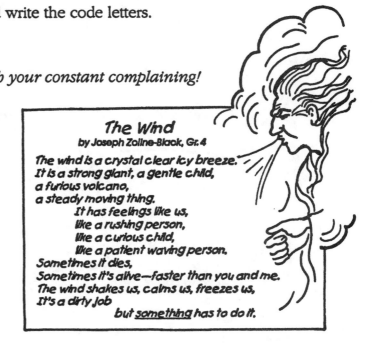

The Wind
by Joseph Zoline-Black, Gr. 4

The wind is a crystal clear icy breeze.
It is a strong giant, a gentle child,
a furious volcano,
a steady moving thing.
　　It has feelings like us,
　　like a rushing person,
　　like a curious child,
　　like a patient waving person.
Sometimes it dies,
Sometimes it's alive—faster than you and me.
The wind shakes us, calms us, freezes us,
It's a dirty job
　　　　but something has to do it.

35. The limerick is out of order! Number the lines in the right order.

_____ Of the dragons so near,

_____ It's just that his suit was too tight!

_____ For months kept refusing to fight.

_____ He didn't have fear

_____ It's strange that Sir Guilford, the Knight

36. Read the poem. Write two more lines with the same form the writer has used.

What I WAS and What I AM
by Sophie DiStephano, Gr. 2

I was a tree but now I'm paper
I was wheat but now I'm bread
I was a stream but now I'm a river
I was a chick but now I'm a chicken
I was a sprout but now I'm the biggest tree in the world
I was nothing but now I am something
I was a loaf of bread but now I'm a crumb

I was _____ but now I'm _____

I was _____ but now I'm _____

Name _____

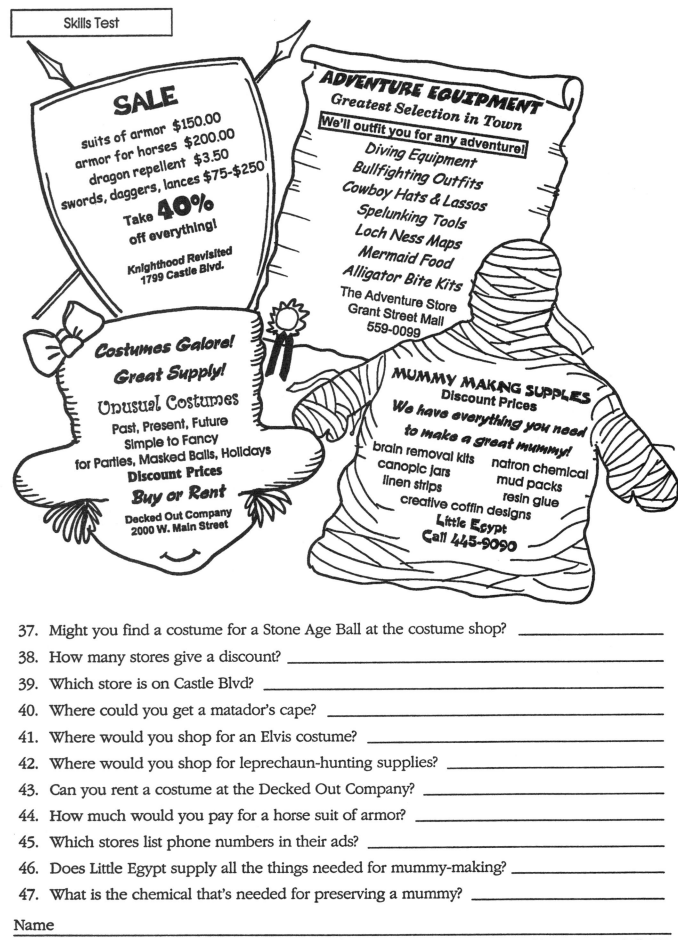

SALE

suits of armor $150.00
armor for horses $200.00
dragon repellent $3.50
swords, daggers, lances $75-$250

Take **40%** off everything!

Knighthood Revisited
1799 Castle Blvd.

ADVENTURE EQUIPMENT
Greatest Selection in Town
We'll outfit you for any adventure!

Diving Equipment
Bullfighting Outfits
Cowboy Hats & Lassos
Spelunking Tools
Loch Ness Maps
Mermaid Food
Alligator Bite Kits

The Adventure Store
Grant Street Mall
559-0099

Costumes Galore!
Great Supply!
Unusual Costumes
Past, Present, Future
Simple to Fancy
for Parties, Masked Balls, Holidays
Discount Prices
Buy or Rent
Decked Out Company
2000 W. Main Street

MUMMY MAKING SUPPLIES
Discount Prices
We have everything you need
to make a great mummy!
brain removal kits   natron chemical
canopic jars   mud packs
linen strips   resin glue
creative coffin designs
Little Egypt
Call 445-9090

37. Might you find a costume for a Stone Age Ball at the costume shop? _____

38. How many stores give a discount? _____

39. Which store is on Castle Blvd? _____

40. Where could you get a matador's cape? _____

41. Where would you shop for an Elvis costume? _____

42. Where would you shop for leprechaun-hunting supplies? _____

43. Can you rent a costume at the Decked Out Company? _____

44. How much would you pay for a horse suit of armor? _____

45. Which stores list phone numbers in their ads? _____

46. Does Little Egypt supply all the things needed for mummy-making? _____

47. What is the chemical that's needed for preserving a mummy? _____

Name _____

Are You Ready?

If you ever plan to do any adventuring in space, you will need to know how astronauts get along. When you head into space, the ordinary environment of life is gone. There is no air, sunshine, day or night, or gravity. When your shuttle takes off, your body will feel squished and squashed. Everything in the world of the astronaut is without gravity. You will have to sleep, move, eat, and stay healthy in a place where everything floats around.

Fortunately, you'll have a space suit made of fifteen plastic layers that supplies you with oxygen and removes carbon dioxide and other waste products. The suit keeps the atmospheric pressure right for your body and keeps you warm. It has a special drink bag and a camera for sending pictures to the cockpit. You'll also have to be hooked up to a portable lavatory to take care of body wastes!

Living without gravity is quite a bit different from your normal life! You'll have to be tied to your bunk at night or use a sleeping suit. Your dinner would float away if it were not securely wrapped in a package. Living without day and night is strange, too. Someone will have to tell you when it's time for you to sleep.

So, what do you think? Sounds thrilling, doesn't it? Do you still want to head off into space?

48. Find one statement that is opinion rather than fact. Circle it.

49. Find two statements that give details to support the idea that living without gravity is strange. Underline them.

50. The author's purpose in writing this was
    a. to give information
    b. to tell about a particular space trip
    c. to warn you not to go to space

51. The main idea is
    a. Space travel is dangerous.
    b. Astronauts need special equipment to deal with different life in space.
    c. Space travel is great fun.

52. Write a title for this piece.

_____
(Title)

Slowly, stealthily, soundlessly she crept across the balcony. Her tip-toe steps were soft as air. No one must see her! No one must hear her! The hush of the night was so huge that any sound would be like crashing thunder splitting the air. Oh, so smoothly, she pulled herself over the railing. Tying the precious bundle to her long rope, she lowered it cautiously to the ground. With just as much care, she eased over the top of the balcony rail and slid herself after it. Once on the ground, she tied the bundle around her waist and vanished into the dark tangles of the vines and bushes. She was never seen again.

Number these in the order they occurred.

____ 53. She tied up the bundle.

____ 54. She vanished.

____ 55. She climbed over the balcony.

____ 56. She lowered the bundle.

57. One characteristic of the main character that the piece shows is:
    a. She is sinister.
    b. She is a hero.
    c. She is careful.

58. The setting of the story is _____

_____

59. What will happen next? _____

_____

_____

60. Write a short summary of the piece.

_____

_____

_____

Name _____

ANSWER KEY

SKILLS TEST

1–5. Student titles will vary. See that student has given an appropriate, accurate title to each: Something such as:
1. The Biggest Painting
2. So Much Music!
3. The Most Sunken Treasure
4. A Productive Painter
5. The Largest Cake Ever
6. Answers will vary some. Most have to do with large numbers or records.
7. longest dancing dragon
8. limbo stick
9. longest dance
10. most exhausting dance
11. 1991
12. Florida
13. Answers will vary.

14. Answers will vary.
15. hearing
16. You usually do not think of "hearing" sun.
17. dog's toenails, heels on dance floor
18. lightning, seashells
19. 3 of these: crashing, cracking, click, snapping, buzzing, boom, scraping, pitter, cracks, whispers, rumble, roar, chopping
20. Answers will vary.
21. mad
22. boring
23. asteroids, boots on Matterhorn, Paul Bunyan chopping
24. terrible, awful, boring
25. person was awakened from a peaceful slumber
26. Every line begins with "I hear."

27. He doesn't like it.
28. P, S, M, A
29. A
30. I
31. M, P
32. P, A
33. S
34. E
35. 4, 5, 2, 3, 1
36. Answers will vary. See that student follows the pattern accurately.
37. yes
38. 3
39. Knighthood Revisited
40. The Adventure Store or Decked Out Company
41. Decked Out Company
42. The Adventure Store
43. yes
44. $120
45. The Adventure Store, Little Egypt

46. yes
47. natron
48. Sounds thrilling, doesn't it?
49. You'll have to be tied . . . *and* Your dinner will float . . .
50. a
51. b
52. Answers will vary.
53. 1
54. 4
55. 3
56. 2
57. c
58. outside a dwelling on and below a balcony
59. Answers will vary.
60. Answers will vary. **Check for accuracy.**

SKILLS EXERCISES

pages 10–11
1. escapade
2. soar
3. antics
4. fraternize
5. scrutinize
6. endeavor
7. venture
8. probe; comb
9. fantasy or mythical
10. great
11. culinary
12. scale
13. treacherous
14. mythical or fantasy
15. ancient
16. foreboding
17. colossal
18. lavish
19. unfathomable
20. future
21. elusive
22. legendary
23. ruins
24. bargain
25. engage
26. gander
27. remote
28. fiercest

page 12
1. ridiculous
2. thrilled
3. cave
4. reached
5. regret
6. damp
7. dangerous
8. break, rest
9. stop
10. complaining
11. upset, bothered
12. evil, scary
Predictions will vary.

page 13
Answers may vary somewhat from those listed below, but should have generally the same meaning.
1. prove
2. make unworkable
3. obey
4. use
5. drinking
6. fatty or greasy
7. trash
8. banned
9. pay attention to given out
10. not allowed
11. touch, change

12. a great amount scolded
13. tickets
14. right away end

page 14
1. d
2. i
3. g
4. h
5. m
6. n
7. l
8. a
9. o
10. e
11. k
12. b
13. f
14. j
15. c

page 15
1. H
2. B
3. D
4. B
5. C
6. D
7. A
8. F
9. G

10. G
11. E
12. E
13. G
14. H

page 16
1. a
2. c
3. c
4. b
5. b
6. c
7. c
8. b

page 17
1. halfpipe (snowboarding), aerial skiing, ski jumping
2. to fly farther
3. halfpipe (snowboarding)
4. 30%
5. downhill racing
6. ski jumping
7. aerial skiing and halfpipe (snowboarding)
8. NA
9. 1996
10. a U-shaped trench of snow
11. 66 yards

page 18
1. b
2. a
3. c

page 19
Answers will vary some. Main ideas should be generally close to these:
Thursday, May 18: I am going to hunt for mermaids, and I'm excited.
Saturday, May 20: Legend says that mermaids were women of Ireland who were banished from earth to the sea.
Tuesday, May 22: Many people believe in the existence of sea serpents.
Friday, May 25: I think I saw a mermaid today.

page 20
Facts are:
Visit *Mir* Space Station
Travel to *Mir* by Space Shuttle
Orbit the Earth—see fantastic sights!
See the 6-port docking system.
Explore the living and working spaces.
Get fitted with your own space suit.
Walk in space.
All food and equipment provided.
Mir means "peace"
We provide training!
STAY 5, 10, or 15 days
We won't keep you as long as we kept Cosmonaut Aleksandr Laveikin. He stayed 326 days!
Mir was launched in 1986 by the Soviet Union.
Today it is maintained by Russia.
Schedule
See your Adventure Company Representative
Health examination required.
Must be at least 25 years of age.

Opinions are:
You'll be so glad you did this!
Astronauts will enjoy your visit!
You'll have fun feeling weightless!
You'll love the food!
No dangers or accidents will occur.
You can afford it!
All astronauts & cosmonauts want a chance to live on *Mir!*

page 21
1. fairies
2. rainbows
3. boas & black panthers
4. dig to the pit of the Earth
5. bunny
6. stars
7. a time machine
8. the prehistoric air
9. anything
10. winged unicorns' backs
11. in your heart
12. c
13. Answers will vary.
14. Answers will vary.

page 22
1. 4 lbs
2. no
3. carabiners
4. tent, carabiners
5. Climber's Shop
6. $59
7. 3910 Abby Lane
8. Climb of Denali
9. Mountain Supply
10. Camping, Ltd.
11. 2
12. 552-9900
13. Mountain Store
14. $75
15. −60°

page 23
1. 107 inches
2. his ox, Babe
3. 47
4-9. Answers will vary.

page 24
Answers will vary.

page 25
1. Georgio's
2. drawings of flying machines
3. Charlie, Alicia
4. *The Last Supper*
5. Charlie
6. Florence
7. Georgio
8. Answers will vary.

page 26
1. The Paleo-Lyths
2. Till the Volcano Blows
3. Be a Little Boulder, Honey
4. I Dino If I Love You Anymore
5. You're As Cuddly As A Woolly Mammoth
6. The Cave Dudes
7. I've Cried Pebbles Over You
8. Terri Dactyl
9. The Cro-Magnon Crooners
10. The Petro Cliff Trio
11. The Hard Rock Arena
12. 5
13. Tommy Shale
14. after dark
15. The Standing Stones

page 27
1. R,P
2. E,M
3. I, M
4. S
5. I
6. E
7. I
8. A, S
9. A
10. I
11. E,M
12. A, P
13. A, P
14. M
15. P
16. A
17. PN

page 28
1, 2, 6, 7,There are many possibilities. Answers will vary.
3. slipped a cut, stabbed
4. one last drop of water
5. could not take another step, could not say a word

page 29
Answers will vary.

page 30
Order of numbers for line placement.
1. 3, 1, 6, 5, 2, 4
2. 2, 5, 4, 3, 8, 1, 7, 6
3. 2, 4, 7, 1, 3, 5, 6

page 31
Order of numbers for line placement:
1. 4, 1, 5, 2, 3
2. 2, 1, 5, 3, 4 or 5, 1, 2, 3, 4
3. 2, 5, 4, 3, 1
4. 1, 3, 5, 2, 4 or 1, 4, 5, 2, 3
5. 5, 1, 4, 3, 2 or 1, 5, 4, 3, 2

page 32
Answers will vary somewhat. This is the general idea of the meaning of the proverbs.
1. Things get wasted when you hurry too much.
2. If you don't act, you may lose your opportunity.
3. Take advantage of an opportunity.
4. If you take care of something right away, it will save work later.
5. There's something good about everything that seems bad.
6. Someone who keeps busy doesn't get stuck.
7. If you don't try something, you'll never gain anything.
8. Fish rot in three days, and people get tired of visitors.
9. Fools don't think before they rush into something; smart people do.
10. If you tell a secret, it won't get kept.
11. Pay attention to what you have, not what you might have.
12. Don't count on something until you have it.
13. Don't change your plan while you're in the middle of it.
14. You can't make someone do what you want them to do.

page 33

Answers will vary somewhat. This is the general idea of the meaning of the proverbs.
1. Are you fooling me?
2. She is acting crazy.
3. We're in trouble.
4. You're not saying anything.
5. Leave me alone.
6. He's boring.
7. Be quiet.
8. I'm going to have to give in to you.
9. I am mad at you about something.
10. Don't tattle on your friends.
11. I slept really soundly.
12. I took a chance.
13. She told a secret.
14. She said something embarrassing.
15. Time goes quickly.
16. I thought the test was easy.
17. The accident was the last thing I could handle.
18. The kids are annoying me.
19. I barely passed.
20. I was shocked.

page 34

Summaries will vary. Check to see that students have a complete, brief summary that contains the main ideas.

page 35

1. F
2. T
3. T
4. T
5. F
6. F
7. F
8. T
9. F
10. Answers will vary.

page 36

Purposes will vary somewhat.
1. c—Purpose: tell readers how Talula deserves to be a star

2. a—Purpose: discourage would-be stars from going to Nashville
3. b—Purpose: inform readers of some news
4. b—Purpose: instruct reader about neon lights

page 37

Answers will vary.

page 38

Students' predictions will vary.

page 39

1. 1
2. 2, 3
3. poor visibility, cold, control in the wind
4. visibility, dampness, control in the wind
5. probably good
6. possibly cancel or postpone the race

page 40

1. Jamie
2. Jo
3. Jeri
4. Jess
5. Jeri

page 41

1. Answers will vary some. These may be noted.
You begin to imagine . . ..
You are nervous, excited, impatient . . .
You trust this rollercoaster . . .
You are sure it will be safe . . .
You don't care how it works . . .
You just want to get on!
You feel like you are flying . . .
You enjoyed every minute . . .
Your stomach feels great . . .
You want to ride again . . .
2–4. Answers will vary.

page 42

Students' judgments will vary. Check the reasonableness of answers.

page 43

Students' questions will vary. Check to see that the questions are fitting the character.

page 44–45

Character descriptions: Answers will vary.
Exact wording of story elements will vary.
Theme: mystery
Characters: Madeline, Countess, Porter, Doctor, Mystery Man, Robber, Mrs. Matisse, Sleeping Man
Setting: Train—Orient Express
Plot: A little girl notices many mysterious things on a train. After the lights go out, a dog and a porter are missing and some other things are changed.
Point of View: third person (narrator who is not a character)

page 46

1. 40 days
2. dries it out
3. 20 or more
4. organs
5. brain
6. putting it in 3 coffins
7. Answers will vary.

page 47

Incorrect details are:
• caught in the depths of a terrible dungeon
• It seems he will have no chance of escape.
• wingless dragon
• back inside the castle
• a worried damsel
• chained to a pillar
• She is waiting for Sir Prance-a-lot.
• Here comes the dashing knight to the rescue!
Rewrite of story will vary. See that students have correct details.

page 48

1. no
2. Zurich, Basil, Bern
3. Drop 2 or Drop 3
4. no
5. Tues and Fri
6. no
7. Drop 2
8. no
9. 2
10. 4

page 49

1. 3
2. 5
3. 1
4. $341,000
5. $370,260
6. guitar
7. car
8. $132,000
9. 6
10. $722,260

page 50

1. Shun Hing Square
2. Petronas Towers
3. Baiyoke II Tower
4. Amoco Building, T & C Tower
5. Empire State Building
6. World Trade Center
7. John Hancock Building
8. Empire State Building
9. Baiyoke II Tower
10. Petronas Towers

page 51

Look at student graphs to see that they show the following amounts.
1. Isabella II—35 years
2. Maria Theresa—40 years
3. Wu Chao—50 years
4. Victoria—64 years
5. Salote—47 years
6. Suiko—35 years
7. Elizabeth I—45 years
8. Elizabeth II—46 years as of 1998
9. Joanna I—38 years
10. Maria I—39 years
11. Wilhelmina—58 years

page 52

Examine student drawings to see that they have followed directions accurately, or have students examine one another's drawings.

page 53

Answers will vary.

page 54

Answers will vary.